MW00893769

MARKETS

MARKETS
From Barter to Bar Codes

Jeanne Bendick
and Robert Bendick

A First Book

Franklin Watts
A Division of Grolier Publishing

New York London Hong Kong Sydney
Danbury, Connecticut

Photographs ©: Archive Photos: 16, 45, 48, 52; Art Resource: 30 (D. Donne Bryant), 13 left, 24, 25 top (Erich Lessing), 18 (Scala), 26 (SEF), 40 (Werner Forman Archive), 41 (Werner Forman Archive, Museum fur Volkerkunde, Berlin), 10; Comstock: 29 (Mario Corvetto); Corbis-Bettmann: 25 bottom, 33, 44, 49; Folio, Inc.: 56 (Cameron Davidson); Monkmeyer Press: 58 (Clay), 60 (Van Etten); North Wind Picture Archives: 13 right, 17, 21, 36.

Library of Congress Cataloging-in-Publication Data

Bendick, Jeanne.
    Markets : from barter to bar codes / Jeanne Bendick and Robert Bendick.
       p. cm. — (A First book)
    Includes index.
    Summary: Tells the stories of markets all over the world, from ancient times to present day.
    ISBN 0-531-20263-1 (lib.bdg.)   0-531-15850-0 (pbk.)
    1. Markets—History—Juvenile literature. [1. Markets—History.] I. Bendick, Robert. II. Title. III. Series.
HF5471.B46 1997
380.1—dc20

                96-41673
                CIP
                AC

CONTENTS

IN THE BEGINNING

Once, people got their food by hunting, fishing, and gathering plants. They made their clothes from the hides of the animals they hunted. Everything they needed was at hand and free, but life was hard. So people began to invent ways to make life easier and more interesting.

They domesticated animals to use for food and wool. They learned to plant and harvest. They invented weaving. They learned to make pottery, plows, boats, and sandals. Some people became farmers or weavers, potters or artists.

Now suppose you are a farmer who needs baskets to store your grain or a toolmaker who needs wool for a blanket.

Wanting to get something you don't have makes you a buyer.

You need to find a seller who has the thing you want.

Nowadays, that's not hard to do. You can go to a store. You can look for advertisements. If you have the money to pay for it, finding what you need or want is usually easy.

Long ago, it wasn't easy at all. There weren't any stores. There weren't any advertisements. There weren't any weights or measures. There was no such thing as money. It took thousands of years to make the kinds of markets that we have today.

It happened like this.

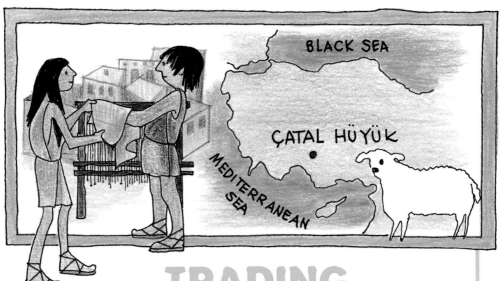

TRADING A THING FOR A THING

TIME: About 6000 B.C.—almost 8,000 years ago
PLACE: Çatal Hüyük, in what is now Turkey

ÇATAL HÜYÜK is the biggest town any-where, crowded with mud-brick houses built against each other.

You are Ala, a young woman living at the end of the time period called the Stone Age. The time is also called *prehistoric*, which means "be-fore written history." In 6000 B.C. nobody has *ever*

Prehistoric paintings are the only records of those times.

written anything. There is no writing to describe events or to tell when they happened. There are no letters and no numerals. There is no way to record business deals. There is no such thing as money.

But you can swap. You can trade something you have for something you need. This is called *barter*.

You want enough cloth to make a dress, but you are not a weaver. Your family does have some extra sheep, so you ask among the weavers in Çatal Hüyük to see if any would trade linen for a sheep. When you find the right weaver you trade your sheep for the cloth.

At first, in bartering, there was no such thing as *equivalency*, which means "things of equal value." You don't say, "But my sheep is worth more than your cloth." You just trade something you have for something you need.

Later, people will see that things and services are not always equal. Then they will bargain until both the buyer and the seller are satisfied. Then the weaver might have to give the cloth, a basket, and a rabbit for Ala's sheep.

Barter is still used in many places and always has been. In some places, money has never been used. In others, when times are hard and money is scarce, barter is a useful way to trade skills and services for goods.

PUTTING IT IN WRITING

TIME: 3000 B.C.—almost 5,000 years ago
PLACE: Sumeria, in what is now Iraq, in the Middle East

YOU ARE A SCRIBE, standing near the riverfront, watching Tamta-Il, a trader, who has come to Uruk, the most important market city in the world. Uruk is in Sumeria, the first great nation of the civilized world, and is located where two great rivers, the Euphrates and the Tigris, come together. Market centers grow in places that are easy for goods and people to get to.

Tamta-Il has come to buy pottery. The streets along the noisy, busy river are lined with workshops. You follow Tamta-Il as he passes furniture makers, then weavers. Next is the street of the potters. He walks along the street, trying to decide which potter will give him the best pots for the best price.

Tamta-Il likes the work of the potter Iptur-Isar, and after some polite talk they squat down to do business.

"I need fifty pots," Tamta-Il says. "How much will they cost? I will pay in gold." He takes a leather bag of small gold nuggets from under his skirt.

When the two men finally agree on the price, the design of the pots, and the delivery date, they have a deal. Iptur-Isar beckons to you, the scribe. The Sumerians have invented writing. Now they can record business transactions, showing what was sold, the names of the buyer and the seller, and the price paid.

The writing is made on soft clay with a wedge-shaped stick called a *stylus*. Writing like this is called *cuneiform,* which means "wedge-shaped." At first, writing was only used for business. Objects were picture symbols. Numerals were arrangements of wedges.

Gradually other kinds of marks were made to stand for words and ideas. Scribes began to keep records of events, dates, and the names of important people.

You use one damp clay tablet to make a bill of sale for Iptur-Isar and another to make a receipt for Tamta-Il. You make still another tablet for the tax collector. Iptur-Isar, who gets the gold, will pay the tax.

When the writing is finished, the clay is baked so there is no way to erase or change the records.

Syrian cuneiform writing

1	Y
2	YY
3	YYY
4	W
5	YYY YY
6	YYY YYY
7	YYY Y
8	YYY YY
9	YYY YYY
10	<

Some cuneiform numerals

Now Tamta-Il has to arrange getting the pottery from Uruk to his home city of Ur, 75 miles (121 km) downstream on the Euphrates River. You go with him until he hires a boat and oarsmen to row his cargo. Tamta-Il agrees to pay the oarsmen two baskets of grain when it arrives safely in Ur. That calls for another tablet, recording when the pots will be delivered to the boat captain, the number of pots, the boat captain's promise of when they will be delivered, and the price Tamta-Il will pay when his cargo arrives in Ur.

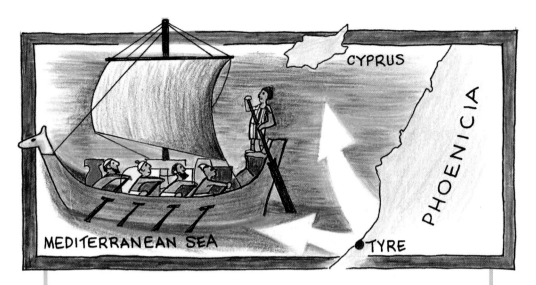

A TRAVELING SALESMAN

TIME: About 800 B.C.—almost 3,000 years ago
PLACE: The port of Tyre, in Phoenicia, in what is now part of Israel, Syria, and Lebanon

 YOU ARE A ROWER in the crew of Psr, a young sea captain, who is supervising the loading of his ship. It's a tubby, wooden cargo ship, heavily built with a bank of oars and a square sail. You are in the port of Tyre, one of the small city-kingdoms that make up the sea-roving, trading nation of Phoenicia. The

The port of Tyre

Phoenicians have built the most seaworthy ships for hundreds of years. They have sailed farther than anyone else—out of the Mediterranean Sea, around Africa, and maybe even to India. They have established new colonies as trading bases.

As each load is stored in the hold, Psr notes it on *papyrus*, a paper made of reeds. He writes in the new alphabet the Phoenicians have invented. The new paper and the new alphabet make doing business easier.

The Phoenicians know what people want to buy. They manufacture all kinds of goods just for trading. They make glassware, metalware, furniture, dyed cloth, and carvings. They have created a movable, seagoing market, buying and selling anything, anywhere, at any time, and at a fair price. Their ships are their markets.

Psr plans to sail to Cyprus, Sicily, Crete, and the Greek Islands. He has a special way of marketing his cargo. He and his crew lay out a display of glass, swords,

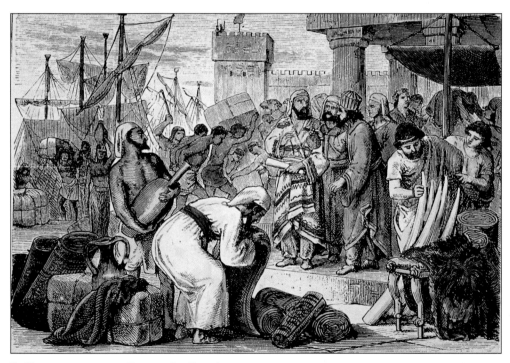

Selling cargo near the waterfront

papyrus, and ornaments on a beach near a town. Then you anchor a short way off and watch.

The people from the town come to look over the wares on the beach. They leave some gold and go away, taking nothing with them. You row Psr back to the beach where he counts the gold. If it seems a fair price he takes the gold, leaves the goods, and you all sail away. If he thinks the amount is too little he leaves the gold; you row back to the boat and wait.

If the townspeople want the goods, they add more gold to the pile. When both sides are satisfied, Psr sails away with the gold, and the buyers leave with what they have bought.

Now the goods for a new voyage are stored below. The wind is fresh, and there is still plenty of daylight.

"Rowers, to your benches," Psr shouts. You and the other rowers maneuver the ship out of the harbor, then set sail on a course to Cyprus. Psr is a Phoenician traveling salesman on his way to sell his wares and explore the ancient world.

**Model of a
Phoenician ship**

COINS
FOR A SLAVE

TIME: 146 B.C.—more than 2,000 years ago
PLACE: The Greek island of Delos

YOU ARE CONAN, a Greek mathematician, a prisoner of war, taken by the Romans. You are frightened and bewildered to find yourself standing naked on a wooden platform next to the auctioneer. Delos, which the Romans have conquered, is a giant slave market. Only one product is sold here—human beings from the places the Romans have conquered. There are hundreds of captives standing and sitting in the hot sun, waiting to be sold. Some are crying, some are afraid, some are angry. Most can't believe what is happening to them.

You stand there, wondering why, since ancient times, people have sold their fellow beings into slavery. You wonder what these captives will be sold to do. Will they be servants or gladiators? Dancing girls, farmhands, miners, or artisans? Some of the Roman buyers will resell the slaves they buy today. Others are buying for their personal use. They will all pay well, and the slave traders will profit.

Now it's your turn to be sold. "He looks old," one buyer calls out.

"Not old, experienced in the noble art of mathematics," the auctioneer says. "Think what an asset he would be to your business! Think what a teacher this mathematician would be for your children! He's a famous scholar!"

"Famous scholar indeed," you mutter to yourself. "A slave!"

"I'll bid two hundred," a stout Roman calls out.

"Two hundred? For this famous scholar?"

"Five hundred!" calls another.

"Seven hundred!"

"A thousand!" calls a dignified, bearded Roman, pulling a heavy purse from under his toga.

"That's better," says the auctioneer. "Any other bids? No? Sold to Marcus Cassius for a thousand!"

A slave market

Marcus Cassius counts out the coins (an invention of the Greeks) and the auctioneer's assistant writes out a receipt. Someone hands you your knee-length tunic and you put it on, glad to be covered again. As you climb down from the platform, your new owner leads you away from this terrible market.

GOODS FROM EVERYWHERE: A ROMAN MARKET

TIME: About A.D. 100—1,900 years ago
PLACE: Ostia, the seaport of Rome

YOU ARE EUDORA, a Greek slave, accompanying your mistress, Claudia, to the market. Claudia is giving a dinner party. She depends on you to carry the baskets of food, to pay the merchants, to count the change, and to check off the shopping list you have written on a wax tablet.

Stone sculpture of a busy Roman shop

Ostia is part of Rome, the greatest city of the Roman Empire, and the street is lined with two-, three-, and four-story apartment buildings. Many shopkeepers live in apartments above their stores. Early every morning the shopkeepers set up business at their stone counters. The dirt street in front of the stores is jammed with shoppers and street venders who are selling sausages, puddings, and spices from wooden trays. Most people are on foot. Rich people ride on litters, carried by slaves. Carts are forbidden in the streets from daybreak until dusk. Before this law was made there were traffic jams, and store-keepers complained that shoppers couldn't get through the streets to do their errands.

Most merchants own their own stores. There are bakers and grocers, pot sellers and oil sellers, and people who make and sell spicy sauces. Some stores sell take-out food from heated containers sunk in the counters. (Not everyone is rich enough to have a kitchen.) Others who have no kitchens take food to the baker to be cooked in the bakery ovens.

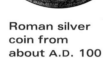

Roman silver coin from about A.D. 100

You and Claudia leave some clothes at the cleaners. You stop at the baker's and then at the butcher's. The butcher weighs a leg of lamb for you. Shoppers don't usually question the weight and the price—government inspectors regularly visit all the shops to check that food is correctly weighed, fairly priced, and of good quality. Prices on some foods are set by law.

"Should we have pigeon or duck, Eudora?" Claudia asks anxiously. "Or maybe octopus or lobster before the meat?"

"I think that will be too much," you say. (You think Romans eat too much.)

The produce market is crammed with fruit and vegetables from all over the Roman Empire. There are beans, celery,

Roman mosaic of a cargo vessel, in ancient Ostia

Street in Ostia, Rome's
harbor town, as it looks
today

cucumbers, squash, lettuce, mushrooms, cabbages, and artichokes. There are figs, plums, pears, and peaches from Persia, cherries from near the Black Sea. There are nuts, berries, and melons.

"Can you carry all this, Eudora?" Claudia asks, after you have bought mushrooms, blackberries, and figs. "And I think we need more bread and some honey to make dessert."

You say, "I'll come back for the bread and honey. And if the clothes have been cleaned, I'll pick them up." And you think to yourself, "And maybe, while I'm out, I'll stop at the bookseller to read a little and then at the wharf to see if there is a ship with news from Greece."

CHOCOLATE MONEY

TIME: About 500—1,500 years ago
PLACE: Tikal, in what is now Guatemala,
in Central America

 YOU ARE IN TIKAL, the most important city of the Mayas. No one in the Americas knows that there are any other civilizations. No one in Europe, Asia, or Africa has any idea that there are people and cities on unknown continents beyond their oceans.

Still, people everywhere are doing the same kinds of things. They are finding, growing, and cooking food. They are selling things they grow or make and buying other things. They are bringing sellers and buyers together in a market.

You are one of a long row of merchants who have set up their awnings along the market walls. You are selling clay pots you have made. Others are selling baskets, brooms, bundles of firewood, salt, fish, beeswax candles, and tobacco. There are peanuts, potatoes, tomatoes, corn, pineapples, and chocolate—things that grew only in the Americas at that time. A butcher is selling rabbits, venison, and turkeys. A cook is selling gourds of stew, which sit steaming over a charcoal fire.

Zak Mak, a farmer, and his wife, May, have also come to the market to sell and to buy. Zak Mak carries a big bag of avocados from his orchard. May has three lengths of beautiful cotton cloth that she has woven on her loom.

Zak Mak and May spread their avocados and weavings on a straw mat near you. Buyers stroll past. Local officials walk through the market, settling disputes and checking prices.

Some shoppers are wearing their currency: shells, carved beads, feathers, and jade. But the most common currency in Tikal is cacao beans. (Cacao is chocolate.) Everyone accepts the beans as money. (Money is whatever the people who make the laws say it is. Today, in

Cacao beans

different places money may be gold or coins, cattle, salt, paper money, checks, or credit cards. In Tikal it's chocolate beans.) In Tikal, if you are rich, you can brew your money and drink it.

Zak Mak and May have good wares and good luck. By the end of the day they have forty-five beans in Zak Mak's rabbit-skin money pouch, and they have bought a new cooking pot from you and a comb for their daughter.

Mayan ruins of Tikal

They will have to pay a tax, either in beans or in work on the king's reservoir, but they will have enough left over to give a party for their daughter's wedding.

TRADE FAIR: A GATHERING OF MERCHANTS

TIME: About 1200—800 years ago
PLACE: The French town of Troyes

YOU ARE REBECCA, bringing your wool from England to the great trade fair that is held in Troyes twice a year.

"If we hadn't gotten here today, I don't think I'd have made it," you groan, helping to lift a big sack of raw wool off one of the pack horses. Your brother stacks it neatly in the stall you have rented in the huge market hall. You have traveled all the way from England, first by boat, then with a larger and larger group of merchants who have come to the fair from all over Europe.

In the Middle Ages, there is no easy way to ship goods from one country to another. But people want goods from all over the known world. So merchants load their wares on pack animals and travel with them. Carts aren't useful—the roads are so bad that carts' wheels get stuck.

The lord at Troyes—the richest landowner, who owns the town—had a grand idea. He built a huge market hall and rents the stalls to merchants from all over, who come with their goods. To encourage them to come to Troyes over the dangerous roads he hires armed guards to protect them from lurking bandits. He also hires jugglers and musicians to entertain in the hall. Lords and princes in other places have copied the idea so merchants travel from one fair to another.

The trade fair is a market for merchants, rather than for ordinary customers.

When you finish putting your wool on display, you leave your brother in charge and start through the hall to see what's for sale. What noise! Mules are braying, horses are neighing, musicians are playing, merchants are shouting to each other in different languages.

Germans have brought furs, lumber, rope, salt, iron,

miels qe ailleurs.

A manuscript page showing trade and industry in the Middle Ages

and amber. The French display wines and tapestries. Traders from the Low Countries—the Netherlands, Belgium, and Luxembourg—have brought fine woolen cloth; some of it is made from wool you brought to the market last year. But it's the wares from Spain and Italy, Africa and Asia that make you gasp.

Beautiful fabrics are flung out for display. Persian rugs glow like jewels. There is glass from Venice and porcelain from China. You stop at the spice counter. You have never tasted pepper and you whisper to yourself, "I'm going to trade a bit of my wool for a taste of that pepper."

Now the market is in full swing. Armor makers and sword makers need iron. Jewelers need gold, silver, and precious stones. Dressmakers need silk. Cloth makers need wool to weave. When you get back to your stall, you find three Italian buyers bidding for your beautiful English wool.

The market works for everybody.

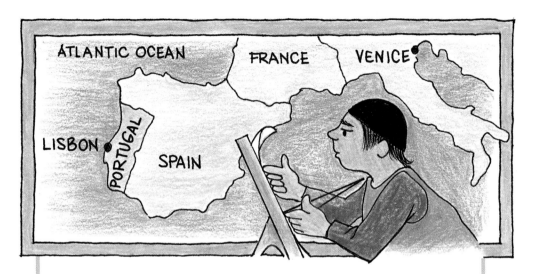

EXPLORING FOR SPICES

TIME: 1525—less than 500 years ago
PLACE: Lisbon, Portugal

YOU ARE BARTHOLEMEU PO, a map-maker who works with other geographers to keep the charts of the known world up-to-date. At the moment you are taking time out to have lunch. As you eat, you think "Ugh! This is the worst-tasting meat and the smell is awful. If only I could afford to buy some of that pepper or nutmeg from the Spice Islands!"

People in Europe wish they had spices to improve the taste of their food. Without refrigeration it is always spoiled and tastes awful. Canning and bottling haven't been invented either. Spices are also good for treating toothaches and other maladies. But who can afford them? Spices are worth their weight in gold.

Venice is the spice-market center of Europe. The merchants there sell salt, pepper, cinnamon, mace, cloves, saffron, and ginger, all bought from Arab traders who sail their ships along secret routes to the pirate-infested Spice Islands and then to the pepper markets of

Loaded camels crossing the Egyptian desert

Calicut, India. Here, European buyers pay a huge tax before they can load the spices on their own ships, sail across the Red Sea to Suez, Egypt, transfer it to camel caravans which cross the desert to Cairo, reload it onto ships that will cross the Mediterranean to Venice, *if* they can evade the Turkish pirates. No wonder pepper and other spices cost a fortune!

You return to your map table where you are making a map for a group of merchants who are organizing an expedition to the Spice

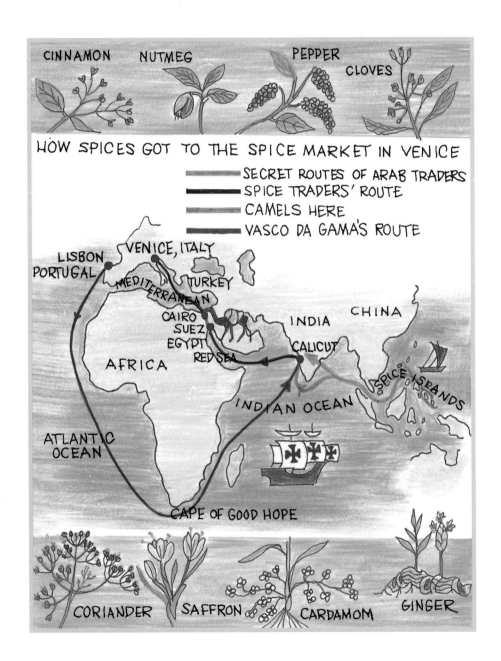

CINNAMON   NUTMEG   PEPPER   CLOVES

HOW SPICES GOT TO THE SPICE MARKET IN VENICE

SECRET ROUTES OF ARAB TRADERS
SPICE TRADERS' ROUTE
CAMELS HERE
VASCO DA GAMA'S ROUTE

LISBON PORTUGAL
VENICE, ITALY
MEDITERRANEAN
TURKEY
CAIRO
SUEZ
EGYPT
RED SEA
AFRICA
INDIA
CHINA
CALICUT
SPICE ISLANDS
INDIAN OCEAN
ATLANTIC OCEAN
CAPE OF GOOD HOPE

CORIANDER   SAFFRON   CARDAMOM   GINGER

Islands. You move your finger over the map, reviewing the routes you have already drawn. You trace the route of Columbus who sailed west, trying to find the spice markets Marco Polo had told of many years before. Instead, he landed in the islands of a new world—no spices there.

You make a correction on the 1497 route of Vasco da Gama, who sailed south from Lisbon. Braving storms and mutiny he beat his way around the Cape of Good Hope, and finally east to Calicut, in India. That makes getting spices a little easier.

Now you begin to draw in the latest route, sailed by Ferdinand Magellan in 1519. Magellan sailed for the king of Spain, who feared that Portugal would have a monopoly on the spice trade.

That three-year adventure is only a line on the map now. Four of his five ships were lost to storms, mutinies, and pirates. Magellan himself was killed, but his mate, Juan Sebastián del Cano, completed the voyage. In 1522, he brought that last ship and only eighteen men into the Spanish port of Seville, loaded with a fortune in spices. The world was being explored so that someday spices would be available to everyone.

A THIEVES' MARKET

TIME: 1637—less than 400 years ago
PLACE: Portobelo, on the Isthmus of Panama

YOU ARE JAMIE HOLTON, an English sailor, and you are standing on the docks of Portobelo, watching the great fleet of Spanish galleons that has come to Portobelo for the annual summer market, famous all over the Caribbean and in Spain itself. The traders on the ships have come to meet the merchants, settlers, and officials who have settled in the Spanish

Main, which was what the mainland of South and Central America was called in those days.

You watch the crowds push their way past Indian and African slaves who are unloading goods onto the wharf—chests of clothing, buttons and buckles, tools, glass and mirrors, bolts of cloth, sacks of flour and spices, casks of oil and wine. Crews are struggling to get horses, cows, and pigs ashore.

The squares behind you are crammed with coffers of gold. Crates of silver bricks have been weighed, recorded, and stacked. You have already looked over the casks of pearls and emeralds, the bolts of wool made from vicuña hair, the rolls of cacao bark and bales of tobacco. The king's soldiers patrol the treasure streets. Nothing is ever stolen from this market.

Golden Inca toucan from the 1400s

But everything here has been stolen. The gold is stolen Inca treasures that have been melted into rough coins and stamped with official seals. You have seen some of the ornaments that were not destroyed and they are wonderfully beautiful. But the Spanish want only the gold itself.

The silver was stolen from the mines at Potosí, in Bolivia. Now the Indians who owned the mines work there as slaves. The silver was carried by mules through the jungle, loaded onto barges, and floated to Portobelo on the Chagres River.

The merchants from the galleons have their wares set out, now. Agents of the settlers and Spanish merchants are wandering among them, fixing prices. You watch a perspiring, overdressed settler who is wearing a huge necklace of gold links. He stops at a display of crystal goblets from England, chooses a dozen, and pays for them by twisting off a link from the gold chain around his neck. The link is weighed on a jeweler's scale and the deal is made. Meanwhile, the treasure is being loaded onto the galleons. Local goods and produce are loaded, too. Exotic materials, fruits, and vegetables bring high prices in Spain.

Silver Inca sculpture from the 1400s

You watch to see which ships have the treasure. Then you slip away from Portobelo and make your way to a hidden cove where the swift privateer *Emily* is moored. You are first mate on the *Emily*.

The *Emily* has letters of marque—a permit issued by

- **41** -

Charles I, king of England, authorizing the *Emily* to capture any enemy ship and its cargo. Spain is an enemy of England. The *Emily* will wait in her cove until the treasure-laden galleons set sail for home, then pounce on one and steal the treasure that Spain stole from the Indians. Portobelo is a real thieves' market.

A FRONTIER STORE

Time: About 1820—less than 200 years ago
Place: The state of Vermont in the new
United States

IT'S EARLY MORNING and you are about to open the door of your general store.

You are Hope Whitehead, and you have the first store in this farming community. Until now, the farmers and their wives had no place to buy even everyday things. They had to repair any tools they had. They made their clothes

Painting of a country store in New England

and even the cloth for the clothes. They made their furniture, their cooking and eating utensils, toys for the children. They grew or made everything they ate.

You look around the store with pride. Beside the everyday things you have pretty fabrics for dresses and woolens for coats. You have china from England and a specially ordered clock from Germany. You have tea and coffee, salt and refined sugar. You have barrels of oatmeal, crackers, and beans. You have guns and gunpowder, bullets, traps, nails, axes, and other hardware.

Sometimes farm families have no money to pay for what they need. You understand that and you wait for harvest time to get paid.

Once a year you go to Boston on the stagecoach to see what you might find for your store in the big city. Otherwise you order by mail. You have to think ahead—it takes weeks for the freight wagon to deliver your orders. You buy some of your stock from peddlers who call regularly, their wagons loaded with everyday needs—pots and pans, needles and thread.

One side of the store is the pharmacy. Your husband is the pharmacist. He has drugs and medicine in big bottles and small jars, in drawers and packets. He orders

Post office in the general store at Old Sturbridge Village, Massachusetts, a reconstructed New England Village

some of them through the mail. The rest he grows or makes himself—remedies for toothaches, backaches, and headaches.

All your children work in the store. They sweep and polish and weigh and wrap and help load and unload the farmers' wagons. Faith, your oldest daughter, is also the postmistress. Every family has its own cubbyhole in the store's post office. The mail coach comes every ten days or so, bringing mail for the community and picking up outgoing mail. There are no radios, newspapers, or telephones so letters are the only way people can keep in touch with their friends and relatives. People pay for their letters when they are delivered.

The store is a kind of clearinghouse for services. If a farmer needs a blacksmith or a new horse, you help arrange the deal. If the farmer's wife wants to have a dress or a hat made, you know someone who will do it for her.

A barber asks if he can set up a barber chair. A neighbor asks if she can bring some of her cooking and serve lunches. People gather at the store to see their friends and exchange ideas about their new country, the United States. Other businesses will grow up around the store and it will become the center of a village.

Now, it's about to open for the day. The bell over the door jingles. "Good morning, Mrs. Smith," you say. "My, that's a lovely bonnet. What can I do for you?"

THE MARKETS
ON MAIN STREET

TIME: 1910—less than 100 years ago
PLACE: Jackfish, Ontario, in Canada

IT'S A SUMMER MORNING and you are Gil Fates, driving your ice wagon along Main Street. Last winter, when the ice on the lake was more than a foot thick, men sawed big blocks of ice, hauled them to a long wooden icehouse, and covered them thickly with sawdust. That ice is still frozen. Early this morning you went to the icehouse, loaded your wagon

Main Street

with blocks of ice, and drove to town to make your deliveries.

On one side of the street are Mugar's Meat Market, Rosa's Vegetable Market, and Page's Hardware. On the other side are Schwartz's Dairy, Herb's Tailor Shop, Cushman's Bakery, the Star Fish Market, and Sam's Grocery Store. Douden's Drug Store and Soda Fountain is on the corner. The stores are all run by families. Some of them are immigrants who worked and saved until they had enough money to start a business. Some live in the buildings above their stores.

Very few people have electric refrigerators. Everyone depends on you to come with your ice wagon and deliver ice to keep food cool and fresh. You deliver to the stores along Main Street and to peoples' homes. Signs in the windows tell how much ice each customer wants that day—from 25 to 100 pounds (11 to 45 kg). When your

Children watching an iceman weighing a large chunk

horse stops at each customer's house, you chip out the right size block, grab your big iron tongs, lift the block of ice out of the wagon, and carry it inside.

All the families in town buy from the stores on Main Street. The storekeepers wait on their customers and wrap their packages. When an order is too big to carry, a delivery boy brings it in a small wagon that is hitched to his bicycle. If a family happens to be short of cash, most of the storekeepers let them buy on credit.

It's a neighborly way of marketing.

A NEW KIND
OF MARKET

TIME: 1931—less than 70 years ago
PLACE: Long Island, New York state

YOU ARE IRV GREENSPAN, just out of college, and you have been hired to write the advertising for a new kind of store—a grocery store that sells directly to the customers at wholesale prices. Wholesale prices are what a merchant usually pays for the goods he buys. Then he marks the price up so he can make a profit when he sells to his customers. But now those customers have very little money to spend.

There is a terrible economic depression and millions of people are out of work. Drought has ruined thousands of farms. The owner of your store has found a way to cut food prices. He has rented a big, old building in a low-rent area, a building that had been used as a ballroom and skating rink. Outside there is plenty of parking space. (Automobiles are becoming common.)

Supermarket dairy counter in the 1930s

The store isn't fancy. It's lit by bare bulbs. On either side of the wide aisles, potatoes, beans, apples, and other produce are piled high in baskets, bins, and barrels. Canned and packaged groceries are stacked in their shipping cartons. The customers pass along the aisles with baskets on their arms, choosing what they want. There are no sales clerks. No service, no delivery, and no credit make it possible for the prices to be much cheaper. Customers like that. Big signs everywhere show the low prices.

The store owner has rented part of the store to other merchants who sell meats, dairy products, baked goods, drugs, cosmetics, auto supplies, and hardware. The customers like being able to buy so many things in one place. There's even a luncheonette. You sit at the counter eating a hot dog and make some notes for the ad you are writing for tomorrow's local newspaper:

It's noisy at the checkout counter where men ring up customers' purchases on big metal cash registers. You listen to a customer as she lifts her full basket onto the counter. "I had to stop because this is all I could carry. This is really a *super* market."

SUPERMARKET!

TIME: Today
PLACE: Your town

YOU ARE COMING INTO a new supermarket, which is so big that you can't see to the ends of it in any direction. You are shopping the world, here—you have 60,000 different items to choose from.

You are wheeling a great supermarket invention, the shopping cart.

The market is controlled by computers. Some are in the store; some are in the supermarket headquarters, miles away. A central computer monitors and controls the temperatures in all the cases. It keeps the right temperatures for vegetables, fish, meat, dairy products, and frozen food. Without refrigeration, the supermarket wouldn't be possible.

Where to start? The produce section is near the entrance. Supermarkets are planned not only for shopping convenience but to tempt you into buying. You buy avocados from Guatemala and apples from New Zealand and dodge the mist of water that showers on the vegetables to keep them fresh.

At the produce department

You pass the flower shop. It's a garden of potted plants and cut flowers from all over the world. Refrigerated cargo planes, trucks, and trains bring flowers and food from everywhere in a hurry—no worries about bad roads or bandits.

You roll your cart through the bakery. Pies, rolls, muffins, and wonderful smells are coming out of the ovens. If you want to, you can buy whole dinners, freshly cooked to take out.

Some supermarkets have independent shops called *concessions.* The concession owners rent space from the market. There could be a bank, a video store, a post office, maybe a pharmacy and a bookstore.

You need pepper, so you push your cart down the spice aisle. There are hundreds of jars and tins of spices from everywhere. Spice traders helped explore the world but spices are nothing special now. There are fifteen kinds of pepper and it doesn't cost much these days.

You look down aisles of household and auto supplies, pottery, and glassware. You pass hats and T-shirts, fishing equipment and gardening tools, furniture and appliances. (Like the Phoenicians, supermarket owners know what people want to buy.)

There's at least one warehouse for *every* supermarket department. Each warehouse is immense. It's so big that the warehouse workers ride up and down the aisles

Forklift operator in warehouse

on motorized forklifts. The warehouse computer tells the forklift operator what to get and where it is. Store computers record what is sold, how many of each item is still in the store, and what needs to be ordered.

Supermarkets can sell things cheaply because they buy things in such huge quantities that they can demand the best prices from the people they are buying from. A cooperative or chain can buy whole herds of cattle, fields of lettuce, orchards of fruit, all the milk and butter from five dairies, all the tuna in a cannery.

If the store is closed at night, that's when workers restock the shelves. If the store is open twenty-four hours, restocking goes on all the time. Once, the great markets were open only a couple of times a year. Now people can shop every day at any hour.

You move on with your cart. In the meat department, everything has been weighed, priced, and packaged. If a market is in an multiethnic neighborhood, it is sure to have the kinds of food its customers like, wherever in the world they come from.

You pick up milk and eggs in the dairy department and look at your shopping list. That's everything, so you head for the checkout counter and empty your cart onto a moving belt that runs past the checker.

On every item except the fresh fruit and vegetables there is a *bar code,* a series of small parallel lines. The bar code tells everything about the item except its price, which may change from week to week as the market advertises specials.

When the checker passes the bar code over an infrared scanner on the counter, the information on the bar code feeds into the store computer, which has been programmed with the current price of every item in the store. The computer matches the product with its price, shows the price on a screen that you can see, and prints the information on the cash register tape.

You can pay with cash or a check or a credit card. (No cacao beans or sheep, please.) A bagger puts your groceries into the cart and you are on your way to the parking lot.

Bar code scanner

People keep inventing new ways to put buyers and sellers together. There are also *super* supermarkets—immense warehouses as big as airplane hangars. Some are called club stores and charge a yearly membership fee, but things are usually a lot cheaper than in other markets. Club stores are for shoppers who buy lots of an item at once. Products are packed by the case or in dozens or in cans and packages that weigh many pounds. Club stores aren't fancy, but they carry a huge variety— food, linens, books, tools, tires, TVs, and almost anything else you can think of.

Other warehouse stores specialize in particular kinds of merchandise—sports equipment or building materials or electronics. You don't have to be a member to buy in these stores. All the giant, no-frills stores depend on selling large quantities with just a small profit on each item.

People who don't want to go to stores at all have other ways of shopping. They can order from catalogs that offer goods from all over the world. They can shop by television or on the Internet. Many kinds of markets are as close as the telephone. But wouldn't you miss squeezing a tomato, smelling the fruit, talking with your neighbors, and being a part of a lively marketplace?

INDEX

ABOUT THE AUTHORS

JEANNE BENDICK has written and illustrated more than one hundred science and information books for children, many of them in the Franklin Watts First Book series. In fact, she wrote the first and the hundredth First Book! Jeanne Bendick is also the author of the elementary grades of a science textbook series. For fun, she devours crossword puzzles and mystery books.

Robert Bendick started in television before it was even on the air and has been a producer/director ever since. He also coproduced and directed *Cinerama* films. He is a member of television's Silver Circle.

Since they began working together, Jeanne and Robert Bendick have produced several books; a television series called *The First Look*, based on the First Books; a number of filmstrip series; and a three-part special for PBS, during which they traveled to markets around the world.

The Bendicks live on the water in Guilford, Connecticut, and sailing an old catboat is one of their pleasures. Other pleasures include movies, Inuit and other primitive art, cooking, travel, and fishing and exploring the Florida Keys. They have two married children.

DATE DUE

GAYLORD			PRINTED IN U.S.A.